W9-BYN-433

# STONE AGE GEOMETRY
# SPHERES

**Gerry Bailey & Felicia Law**
Illustrated by
**Mike Phillips**

# STONE AGE GEOMETRY

## Crabtree Publishing Company
www.crabtreebooks.com
1-800-387-7650

**Published in Canada**
616 Welland Ave.
St. Catharines, ON
L2M 5V6

**Published in the United States**
PMB 59051, 350 Fifth Ave.
59th Floor,
New York, NY 10118

Published in **2014 by CRABTREE PUBLISHING COMPANY.** All rights reserved. No part of this publication may be reproduced, stored in a retrieval system, or transmitted in any form or by any means, electronic, mechanical, photocopy, recording or otherwise, without the prior written permission of the copyright owner.

Printed in Canada/032014/MA20140124

**Authors:** Gerry Bailey & Felicia Law
**Illustrator:** Mike Phillips
**Editor:** Crystal Sikkens
**Proofreader:** Anastasia Suen
**End matter:** Kylie Korneluk
**Production coordinator and**
    **Prepress technician:** Samara Parent
**Print coordinator:** Margaret Amy Salter

Copyright © 2012 BrambleKids Ltd.

**Photographs:**
Cover - Dimitri Melnik Title page - Dimitri Melnik Pg 2 – Gerard Lacz images / Superstock Pg 3 – David M. Schrader Pg 5 – (tl) Kitch Bain (tr) Vitaly Korovin (bl) Le Do (br) Volodymyr Krasyuk Pg 7 – (t) Four Oaks (bl) Derick W. Blake (br) Peter Elvidge / Shutterstock.com Pg 9 – (t) Roland Spiegler (m) orxy (bl) SashaS (bm) Kasia (br) Kallash K Son Pg 11 – (t) Panos Karapanagiotis (bl) Johnbod – en.wikipedia.org (br) Robert Huggett – it.wikipedia.org Pg 13 – (t) Brad Wynnyk (m) Stephen Coburn (b)Oleg_Mit Pg 15 – (tl) marcovarro (tr) Dimitri Melnik (bl) schankz Pg 17 – (l) Vividz Foto (r) totophotos Pg 19 – (tl) Aspect3D(tr) Ali Ender Birer (bl) PRIMA (br) Konstantin Sutyagin Pg 21 – (t) ekawatchaow (ml) Vtls (mr) SeanPavonePhoto Pg 23 - (t) David Harber www.davidharber.com (bl) Zinaida (br) NattikaPg 25 – (top from l-r) titelio, Leo, valzan, rangizzz (b) Christie's Images Ltd. / Superstock Pg 26 – (from top clockwise) Vaclav Volrab, Sophie Bengtsson, valzan, godrick, Anrey Pg 27 – (from top clockwise) Evgeniapp, WimL, Kuzmin Andrey, mmmx, concept w Pg 29 – (from l-r) Gencho Petkov, vetkit, maxim ibragimov, Harmonia, DeAgostini / Superstock Pg 31 – (tl) Klettr (tr) vadim kozlovsky (ml) Stephen Gibson (mr) photosync (b) Astronoman
All images are Shutterstock.com unless otherwise stated

**Library and Archives Canada Cataloguing in Publication**

Bailey, Gerry, author
    Stone age geometry: Spheres / Gerry Bailey, Felicia Law ; illustrator: Mike Phillips.

(Stone age geometry)
Includes index.
Issued in print and electronic formats.
ISBN 978-0-7787-0510-9 (bound).--ISBN 978-0-7787-0516-1 (pbk.).--ISBN 978-1-4271-8235-7 (html).--ISBN 978-1-4271-9005-5 (pdf)

    1. Sphere--Juvenile literature.  2. Geometry--Juvenile literature. I. Law, Felicia, author  II. Phillips, Mike, 1961-, illustrator  III. Title.

QA491.B353 2014          j516'.154          C2014-900424-9
                                             C2014-900425-7

**Library of Congress Cataloging-in-Publication Data**

Bailey, Gerry, author.
 Stone age geometry: Spheres / Gerry Bailey & Felicia Law ; illustrated by Mike Phillips.
    pages cm. -- (Stone age geometry)
 Includes index.
 ISBN 978-0-7787-0510-9 (reinforced library binding : alk. paper) -- ISBN 978-0-7787-0516-1 (pbk. : alk. paper) -- ISBN 978-1-4271-8235-7 (electronic html : alk. paper) -- ISBN 978-1-4271-9005-5 (electronic pdf : alk. paper)
 1. Sphere--Juvenile literature. 2. Geometry, Solid--Juvenile literature. I. Law, Felicia, author. II. Phillips, Mike, 1961- illustrator. III. Title.

 QA483.B35 2014
 516.156--dc23
                                             2014002077

# LEO'S LESSONS:

# MEET LEO

Meet Leo,
the brightest kid
on the block.

So that's Leo!

Bright as in IQ
off the scale,
inventive as in
Leonardo da Vinci
inventive, and
way, way ahead
of his time....

Block as in
Stone Age block.
Stone Age as in
30,000 years ago.

Then there's Pallas.
Leo's pet.

Pallas is wild and he's OK with
being called Stone Age, too; after
all, his ancestors have been around
for millions of years. And that's
more than you can say for Leo's!
You won't see many Pallas cats
around today, unless you happen to
be visiting the icy, cold wasteland of
Arctic Siberia (at the top of Russia).

# A GAME OF SOCCER

"Its a day off," says Leo.

"A day off what?" asks Pallas.

"A day off mathematics, brainy inventions, and learning stuff," says Leo.

"We're playing soccer instead."

Pallas is fine with soccer. He certainly prefers soccer to math.

All he ever does in math is all the tough parts that Leo doesn't want to do himself, such as testing Leo's flying machine or dragging his loaded sled around.

Pallas is the goalie.

Leo kicks the ball right past him into the net.

"Goal!" he cries.

"Pallas, you're supposed to stop the ball from going in the net," says Leo.

Pallas tries again.

"Goal!" calls Leo again.

## WHAT IS A SPHERE?

A sphere is a solid shape that is perfectly round.

Solid shapes are known as three-dimensional, or 3-D, shapes.

A sphere has a completely curved surface.

A ball is a sphere.

*Balls that are used in sports and games are spheres.*

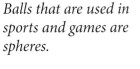

## DIFFERENT DIMENSIONS

One-dimensional(1-D) shapes are a line. One-dimensional shapes only have length.

Two-dimensional (2-D) shapes have length and width. A rectangle is a 2-D shape.

Three-dimensional (3-D) shapes have length, width, and height. They are known as solids.

*Many familiar fruits are in the shape of a sphere.*

# ROLLING SPHERES

"Help me make a head," says Leo.
  "A head?" asks Pallas.
  "A head for my snowman." says Leo. "Here, it's quite simple. Take a small snowball and roll it around in the snow. Snow is sticky so it will gather more and more snow until it's really big. I need a really big head."

  "Right," says Pallas, "as if it's that easy."

Pallas starts with the small snowball.
He pats it into a round sphere shape. Then he carefully starts to roll it along the ground.

He rolls and rolls and rolls...

Leo finally finishes the snowman's body.
He looks around for Pallas and calls out,
"Pallas. I'm ready for the snowman's head."

But Pallas is nowhere to be seen.
Nor is the head.

But down at the bottom
of the hill, there's a large ball
of snow...

## SPHERES ROLL

It is hard work dragging a heavy object along the ground. The object rubs against the rough surface of the ground underneath. This rubbing is caused by a force called friction.

Friction is a force that holds back the movement of a sliding object. But there is less friction if the object has a smooth surface. And there is even less friction if only a small part of an object is touching the ground.

A sphere is smooth, and it touches the ground in just one small spot on its surface.

That's why spheres roll smoothly over the ground.

*Dung beetles roll balls of dung many times their own weight.*

## Dung rollers

*Dung beetles eat **dung** that has been dropped on the ground by animals. They use their strong sense of smell to look for droppings. Once they find some, a dung beetle will form the dung into a sphere and roll it away. Sometimes another dung beetle will try to steal the dung ball, so the dung beetle has to move fast!*

*Most dung beetles can roll a ball up to ten times their weight. That might seem like a lot, but there is one kind of dung beetle that can roll 1,141 times its own body weight. That's the same as an adult pulling six double-decker buses full of people!*

*Lawn bowling is a sport in which the players compete to roll balls called bowls close to a smaller ball called a jack.*

# LAYER BY LAYER

"Why are you rubbing that stone?"
asks Pallas.
"I'm polishing it so it shines," says Leo.
"The more I polish, the shinier it will
be. Come and help."

Pallas helps Leo rub the stone. They
rub away all the rough parts, but it's
slow, hard work.
"How long do we have to do this?"
Pallas asks.

"For about a million years," says Leo. "That's
how long it takes most rocks to be rubbed
smooth. It's already taken years and years
of rain and wind and blowing dust to
scratch off the rough surface and make
it this smooth."
"So this stone used to be much
bigger?" says Pallas.

"Oh yes," says Leo. "And if we keep on
rubbing, one day it will be the size of a
grain of sand."

"I must go!" says Pallas.
"I'd like to stay and help,
but I just remembered I
have something to do..."

## Erosion

Rubbing can change the shape of an object. Rubbing the sharp edges and corners off a piece of stone makes it round. We call this action erosion.

Over a long period of time, the constant force of the rain, wind, or sea will cause erosion. Even an object that is moving through the **atmosphere** will be rubbed by the air and slowly eroded. Most erosion wears an object into a smooth, rounded shape, or a sphere.

The Moeraki boulders in New Zealand are giant spherical rocks. Many are over 7 feet (2 meters) across and are almost perfect spheres. They have been eroded into this shape by the waves.

This rock has been eroded into a sphere by the forces of wind and dust.

A pearl is a sphere that grows in an oyster shell. An oyster is a mollusk, which is a kind of shellfish.

An onion is a sphere-shaped vegetable that grows layer by layer. Each layer is actually a leaf wrapping around the central bud. If you cut an onion in half you can see how it has built up its spherical shape.

## Pearls

There is one animal that does the opposite of erosion. It adds layers of material. When a tiny intruder or parasite enters the shell of a **mollusk** and makes its home there, it rubs on the mollusk's smooth lining. To stop the irritation, the mollusk oozes out a special mixture that covers the intruder. This builds layer by layer and finally hardens into a pearl.

# ANCIENT SPHERES

"Another ball?" says Pallas. "What are you going to do with this one?"

"This," says Leo, "is going to be stuck on the pole. It is the **mace** head for tonight's ceremony, and now that you're here, you can pick up that **flint** and help me shape it."

Leo shows Pallas how it has to be chipped and shaped all over with knobs.
 "A bumpy mace head," says Pallas. "What ceremony needs a bumpy mace head?"

"It's the hunt," says Leo. "This ball is the sacred one that stays here in the village. But then we'll make lots more to throw during the hunt. See? When they're fired from a slingshot like this, they really go far."

"Did I hear you say hunt?" asks Pallas.
"Yes," says Leo. "Ok, I'm outta here!" says Pallas.
"Where are you going?" asks Leo.
"To sharpen my teeth and claws with a flint," says Pallas.

## The stone spheres of Costa Rica

This amazing collection of more than 300 stone balls was discovered in various locations in Costa Rica. Locally, they are known as "Las Bolas." It is thought that they were carved by an **extinct** tribe called the Diquis, and they are sometimes referred to as the Diquis Spheres.

## Carved spheres

Hundreds of carved stone spheres, roughly 3 inches (7.6 centimeters) in **diameter**, have been found in Scotland. They are about 2,000 years old. Many are carved with knobs. No one knows exactly what they were used for. Perhaps they were weapons or ceremonial maces carried by tribal leaders.

Stone spheres of Costa Rica

This stone sphere, carved with knobs, is in the British Museum, in London, U.K.

The Klerksdorp Spheres have been collected by miners from 3-billion-year-old rock deposits in South Africa. They were formed into small sphere shapes naturally in the rocks by heat and erosion.

# THROWING THE BALL

"There!" says Leo. "What do you think of it?
It's my latest invention.
A really big throwing
machine."

"What are you throwing?"
asks Pallas. "It must be
something pretty big."

"Yep!" says Leo. "YOU!"

"Hmm!" says Pallas. "How far
are you planning to throw
me and where am I supposed
to land?"

"It's an experiment," says Leo.
"So I don't exactly know the answer.
But I will know—after the experiment."

"It might be better," Pallas suggests, "to
experiment with something that isn't
me. That boulder for example."

"It's heavier and it won't go as far,"
Leo says.

"But it won't yell with pain and make a fuss when it
lands," says Pallas.

## PARABOLA

When a ball is thrown in the air, it follows a path that first goes upward then downward. This shape is called a parabola.

The ball will start to fall when it reaches the top of the curve. This point at the top of the parabola is known as the vertex.

The vertex happens halfway between the place where the ball takes off (A) and the place where it lands (B).

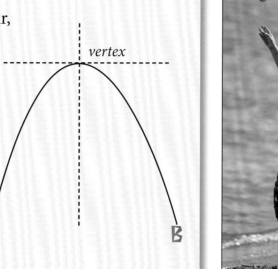

*If you throw a ball, it always follows the path of a parabola.*

## Catapults and cannons

*In olden days, the **catapult** was a fearsome weapon. It could be used to hurl huge boulders at the walls of an enemy's castle and make them crumble. It was important to know how heavy the boulder was, how far the catapult would throw it, and the force of the impact it would make when it landed.*

*Heavy balls were fired from cannons to create the same kind of damage. Cannonballs were made into spheres from stone and sometimes iron.*

*Huge balls were fired from these old cannons.*

*This old catapult would have fired huge boulders at the enemy.*

# ALL DIRECTIONS

Leo is blowing dandelion seeds.
"Why?" asks Pallas. "Why are you blowing dandelion seeds?"

"It's math," says Leo. "See how the seeds are all attached to a stalk in a sphere shape. That's because they will be ready to fly off soon, and when they do, they want to fly away in every direction."

"Wow!" says Pallas. "Like a seed explosion."

"That's it!" says Leo. "If they all went in the same direction, they'd land together and have to fight for that piece of ground. This way, they'll all land somewhere different and get their own space."

A sphere-shaped plant, such as this dandelion head, has the best chance of scattering its seeds across a large area.

## Bubbles make spheres

A bubble is a thin film of soapy water. Most of the bubbles that you see are filled with air.

A soap bubble has a soft skin that holds everything in. The skin has three layers. A thin layer of water is sandwiched between two layers of soap molecules. The soap molecules always turn to face the water so they are pushing inward and outward and holding the bubble's round shape.

At the same time, the air inside the bubble is pushing outward in every direction. This is also helping to make the sphere shape.

No matter what shape a bubble has at first, it will always try to become a sphere.

Bubbles form when water boils.

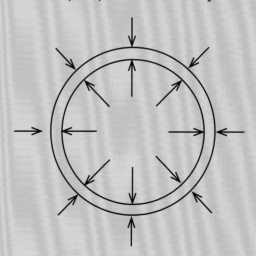

15

# BALLOONS

"Here we go!" says Leo. "Hold on to the basket. You don't want to fall out!"

Pallas certainly doesn't want to fall out. He isn't certain he wants to be here at all... rising off the ground in a basket... with a fire blowing hot air into some kind of huge round balloon... and the whole thing carrying him away into the sky.

"Don't worry!" calls Leo. "The balloon will keep going up as long as we keep it full of hot air. Hot air is lighter than cold air so it has to rise."

The balloon is certainly full. And it is certainly rising. It is a great sphere floating in the sky. The wind carries it this way and that.

Pallas doesn't feel so good.
"Can we go down now?" he asks.

"OK," says Leo. "I think I remember how to do it..."

*Helium gas helps the balloon rise because it is a light gas and the air around it is heavier.*

## Farmyard flight

*Can you believe that a sheep, a duck, and a rooster were the first passengers to ever travel in a hot air balloon?*

*The French brothers Jacques and Joseph Montgolfier wanted to invent an aircraft that could use smoke and heat to lift it off the ground. On September 19, 1783, they managed to launch a balloon made from paper and cloth. They burned some straw, wool, and dried horse manure underneath the balloon. The straw made enough heat to keep the balloon in the air. The wool and manure made lots of smoke that kept the flame low, so the balloon didn't catch fire.*

*The brothers tested their invention using the sheep, duck, and rooster. The paper balloon floated up into the sky and landed safely after eight minutes. A few months later, the brothers demonstrated the first flight with human passengers.*

# EARTH'S SPHERE

"What's the biggest sphere you know?" asks Pallas.
"We're sitting on it," says Leo. "Well, there may be
bigger ones but this is the biggest I know about."

"You mean we're sitting on a huge sphere?"
"Yep," says Leo. "A big sphere that's spinning
around and around in space."

"Ow!" yells Pallas. "Hold on to me. I might slide off."

"You won't," says Leo. "There's this force called
gravity that is holding you down. It's pulling us
both down and holding us on the surface. We're
not going to slip off, I promise."

"Still, I'd rather hold on to something," says Pallas.

## A SPHERE'S FRAME

If you made a frame of a sphere it would look like this.

Curved lines would run from the top to the bottom of the sphere.

Curved lines also run around the sphere. The longest of these runs around the widest part of the sphere at its center.

The lines then get shorter and shorter as they move toward the top and bottom points.

*The Sun and Moon look like spheres when seen from Earth.*

*Seen from space, Earth looks like a perfect sphere.*

*LONGITUDE AND LATITUDE*
*Mapmakers have given Earth imaginary lines that form a frame around it to help identify the location of places on Earth. Measured in degrees, the lines along its width are called latitude. The lines along its length are called longitude.*

*The equator is a line that runs around the middle of Earth. It lies at 0 degrees latitude. Latitude measures how far north or south an object is on the planet.*

*Lines of longitude all run from the North Pole to the South Pole. They measure how far east or west an object is.*

19

# HALF A SPHERE

"What is it?" asks Pallas.
"Dunno!" says Leo. "But it's moving."

The shape lumbers toward them.
    It gets bigger and bigger.
    "It's a big round shell with feet," says Leo.

"I'm out of here!" says Pallas. "It looks like
    a tough guy to me, with that hard case on
    its back. Does it bite?"

"I think it's friendly," says Leo.

It is! Leo climbs on its back.
"Come on Pallas," he calls. "Come and join me."

The tortoise looks at Pallas.
Pallas looks at the tortoise.
Maybe if he had a protective
shell too, he might feel safer.

Some tortoises have a shell that is almost a perfect half sphere.

*Half an apple makes a half-sphere shape.*

## SYMMETRICAL SPHERES

A sphere is symmetrical. No matter which way you turn it, it always looks the same. And if you cut it in half, the two halves will always be perfect mirror images of each other.

## *Dome of the Rock*
*The Dome of the Rock in Jerusalem, Israel, is a Muslim shrine that is built over a sacred stone. The dome at the top of the Dome of the Rock is covered with gold. It is a famous and impressive sight.*

*The Dome of the Rock can be seen from all over the city of Jerusalem.*

## HALF SPHERES

A hemisphere is half a sphere. When a sphere is cut through the center it forms two equal hemispheres. The face of a hemisphere is a perfect circle.

The radius of the sphere is the distance from the center of the face to its circumference, or outer edge.

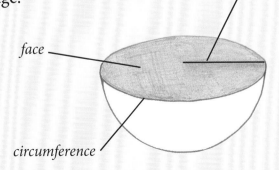

radius

face

circumference

21

# DIVIDING THE ORANGE

"Have a piece of orange, Pallas," says Leo. "No thanks," replies Pallas. "Oranges are not really a cat thing."

"That's too bad," says Leo. "They're packed full of healthy vitamins."
"So are mice," says Pallas.

"Anyway, it's just as well. I need all the pieces to share with the tribe's soccer team today. There are 11 players on the team, but I only have ten sections in my orange. I'll be one piece short."

"Perhaps one of the players should be a cat," suggests Pallas. "Then you'd have enough."

"Brilliant!" says Leo. "You can play on the team tonight and then I'll have enough orange pieces to go around."

## SECTIONS

A piece that is cut out of a sphere so that the cutting line passes down the center is known as a section.

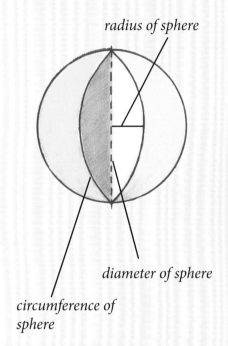

*radius of sphere*

*diameter of sphere*

*circumference of sphere*

A section shows three measurements: you can see the diameter, the radius, and the circumference of the sphere.

*The English sculptor David Harber made this spherical sculpture with a section cut out as a piece of outdoor art.*

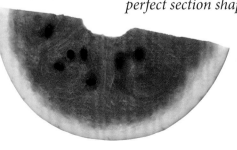

*A slice of melon is a perfect section shape.*

*A peeled orange divides naturally into equal-sized sections.*

23

# SQUASHED SPHERE

"That's it!" says Leo. "Ruined!"
"I only sat on it," said Pallas.

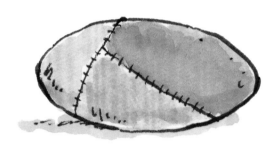

"And you squashed it," says Leo. "It was a perfectly good soccer ball, and now it's a squashed soccer ball."

"We can still play with it," says Pallas.

"No, we can't," says Leo. "It won't roll for a start. How can we play soccer with a ball that won't roll?"

"Well, we could run around with it," says Pallas. "Look, I'll pick it up and run off with it, like this."

"Oh no, you don't," says Leo. "That's MY ball. Hey! Put it down!"

He jumps on Pallas and wrestles with him. They roll all over the ground.
"I got it!" calls Leo. "And I'm going to run off with it now, if you don't stop me!"

"Great game," says Pallas.

## SPHEROID

A "squashed" sphere is known as a spheroid.

It is shaped like a sphere, but is not perfectly round.

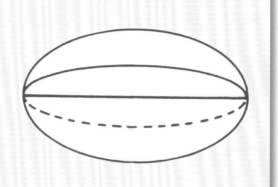

*A watermelon*

*A balloon*

*A football*

*Eggs*

## Earth Is Not Round

*Planet Earth is not perfectly round. It may seem round when viewed from space, but our planet is actually a "bumpy" spheroid.*

*It was the English mathematician and astronomer Isaac Newton, who lived more than 200 years ago, who first suggested that Earth was not perfectly round. Instead, he suggested it was an "oblate spheroid"—a sphere that is squashed at its poles and swollen at the equator. He was correct. Earth is about 13 miles (21 kilometers) wider around its middle than it is from pole to pole.*

*Isaac Newton lived in England in the mid-1600s to early 1700s.*

# CYLINDERS

"That's not a sphere," says Pallas.

"I know," says Leo. "I want something round and tall that I can close with a lid—and a sphere won't do. So I'm using a cylinder."

"What is it?" asks Pallas.

"A tank!" says Leo. "We're going to fill it with water, put the lid on so it stays clean, and then let the water out again."

"How?" asks Pallas. "And why?"

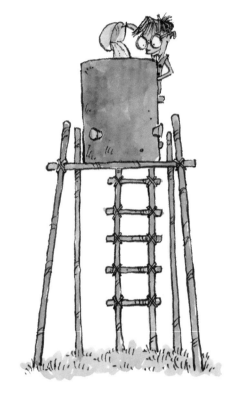

"Stand there!" says Leo.

He takes the corks out of the holes in the sides of the cylinder and water sprays everywhere.

"Eek!" yells Pallas. "I'm soaking wet!"

"We're taking a shower," says Leo.

"I'm a cat!" says Pallas, as he escapes the splashes. "If I want to wash myself I have a perfectly good tongue."

## CYLINDER

A cylinder is a different kind of rounded shape that is also three-dimensional, or solid.

It is made up of a curved surface attached to a circular base at either end.

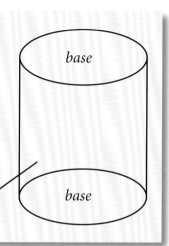

*base*

*base*

*curved surface*

*Cylinders come in all shapes and sizes. They are mostly used as containers.*

*gas cylinder*      *bottle*      *batteries*

*can*

## TUBE

A tube is a long hollow cylinder, often filled with air or liquid. A tube is a curved surface that has no circular base at its ends.

Tubes are used for moving liquids from place to place.

*A straw is an example of a tube.*

## Cylinder seals

*A cylinder seal is a cylinder engraved with a "picture story." Some have birds and animals carved in their surface. Some show people busy at work.*

*The seals were used thousands of years ago in ancient Mesopotamia, which is part of modern Iraq. They were used as jewelry and even as magic charms. They were also used as actual seals, to close letters and mark clay documents as genuine records.*

*The seal on the right made the imprint below when it was rolled over a piece of clay.*

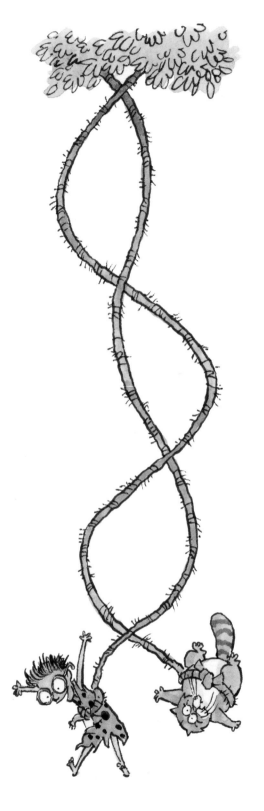

# BENDY HELIX

"Whee-e-e-e-e-e!" screams Leo.

"Whee-e-e-e-e-e!" screams Pallas.

The two are twisting down from the trees, spinning and coiling like two daring bungee jumpers.

It had been Leo's idea that they find two long vines high in the trees above.

"Tie the end around your waist," he told Pallas, "then spin on the branch. That's right. Keep turning."

"I'm dizzy!" Pallas complained.

"That's the fun!" said Leo. "You're winding and winding one way, then when you jump, you'll unwind and unwind the other."

"Jump?" said Pallas, looking down at the ground below. "No one said anything about jumping!"

"Well, how else will the vine uncoil?" said Leo. "Now jump!"

## HELIX

A helix is a 3-D curve. It is the same as a spiral but it has length, width, and height.

A helix is a coiled shape.

*A snail's shell forms a spiral. A spiral is a 2-D curve. A helix is a 3-D spiral.*

*A twirling pattern of lights forms a perfect helix.*

*Slinky toys are based on a helix shape.*

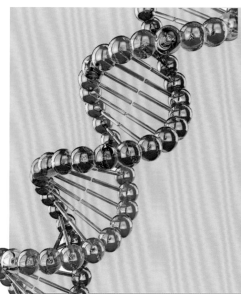

## The helix that is you

*Each person has a special set of instructions about how each cell in their body should behave. The set of instructions is a kind of code.*

*The code is contained in a substance found in the cells that is called deoxyribonucleic acid, or DNA. DNA is too small to be seen without a powerful microscope, but it looks like two spirals twisted together in a double helix shape.*

# SPHERES AROUND US

There are spheres all around us. They are almost always things of beauty, such as sparkling raindrops or bright berries, fruits, and flowers. A sphere is also the shape of many containers and household items. It is a favorite shape used by artists and sculptors. And of course, balls are used in many of the sports and games we play.

*Waterdrops form with a sphere-shaped skin.*

*Round seeds will roll farther and spread more easily.*

*Ripe berries attract birds who eat them and scatter the seeds in their droppings.*

*Spherical seed heads will scatter in all directions and help to grow new plants in different areas.*

*Sphere-shaped peas fit snugly in a pod.*

# LEARNING MORE

## OTHER BOOKS

*Basher Science: Algebra and Geometry*
by Dan Green and Simon Basher, Kingfisher (2011).

*Mummy Math: An Adventure in Geometry*
by Cindy Neuschwander, illustrated by Bryan Langdo.
Square Fish (2009).

*Captain Invincible and the Space Shapes: Three Dimensional Shapes*
by Stuart J. Murphy, illustrated by Remy Simard
HarperCollins Publishers (2001).

*Cubes, Cones, Cylinders, & Spheres*
by Tana Hoban, Greenwillow Books (2000).

## WEBSITES

Get the facts on the shere and its properties at this entertaining website:

http://www.kidsmathgamesonline.com/facts/geometry/spheres.html

Find a variety of games and activities with geometry themes.

www.kidsmathgamesonline.com/geometry.html

This website provides information on shapes and their properties.

www.mathsisfun.com/geometry/index.html

## KEY WORDS

A sphere is a solid, three-dimensional shape that is perfectly round.

When a ball is thrown in the air, it follows an upward then a downward path. This shape is called a parabola.

A hemisphere is half a sphere.

A helix is a 3-D curve. It is the same as a spiral but it has length, width, and height.

A piece that is cut out of a sphere so that the cutting line passes down the center is known as a section.

A "squashed" sphere is known as a spheroid.

A cylinder is a kind of rounded shape that is also 3-D, or solid. It has a flat top and bottom and a curved surface.

# GLOSSARY

**atmosphere** The air surrounding Earth

**catapult** An ancient weapon used for throwing objects, such as stones, at enemies

**diameter** A line passing through the center of a circle or sphere that goes from one side to another

**dung** The poop of an animal

**extinct** No longer existing

**flint** A hard dark quartz that produces a spark when struck by steel

**mace** A heavy spiked club used as a weapon in the Middle Ages

**mollusk** An animal that has a hard shell and a soft body, such as snails, clams, and octopuses

# INDEX